Recognized Expert Status:

Exponential Marketing

by

Scott A. Gardner

For my wife, Arlene Staubsinger, Ph.D.
Without you, I can do nothing.
With you, I can do anything.

Contents

Introduction

Developing and implementing RecEx (Recognized Expert) Status does not happen over night. It is not a "get rich quick" scheme. Rather, it is a tool you add to your marketing kit that amplifies your other efforts. Used properly, RecEx Status can increase your reach, your credibility – and your profits – exponentially. Used poorly, you risk running what is essentially an anti-marketing campaign.

Like any tool, you get out of RecEx Status benefits comparable to what you put in. Like any tool, you can purchase a cheap version for a little money, or a quality version by investing more. And like any tool, no matter which version you have – cheap or quality – it doesn't help if you never put it to use.

When you develop and use RecEx Status, you are literally adding leverage to your other efforts. Like a long lever over a fulcrum, RecEx Status amplifies the force you get from a given amount of effort.

This book is brief and to the point. I've tried not to add any fluff. It explains the definition and principles behind RecEx Status. We also cover the benefits from using your hard-won status.

I hope you find the information here helpful, as well as eye-opening. After you've read through this book, please register your copy here. You'll receive a Welcome email, and then only get emails when there's a major update to the info.

Thanks for reading! I wish you health, happiness and prosperity.

Definition And Benefits

Definition

People complain to one another. A lot. And in our society,
when they do, the people listening often offer up solutions. They
mention the people they know or have heard of that can help
alleviate the pain. That's very general, so let's give some better
examples.

> *Adam and Bob are talking over a couple beers
> in Adam's basement. Adam points to a dark
> spot on the ceiling.*
>
> *"I've got a leak somewhere up there, and it's
> ruining my ceiling. I've gotta get that fixed."*
>
> *"That sucks," says Bob. "I had the same
> problem a while back. Wally from Wally's
> Plumbing came over and fixed me up. It took a
> couple days, but it hasn't leaked since. I'll
> email you his contact info when I get home."*

Here's another.

> *Larry and Vanessa are in a meeting, discussing
> solutions for some of the problems their
> company is facing.*
>
> *"We need to find out why those bearings in the
> new wheels are giving out so quickly. We need
> to find an engineering company that can study
> them and help us find an answer," says Larry.*
>
> *"I found a video on line," says Vanessa. "This
> guy is explaining his company's testing
> procedures. It looks pretty good. You should
> watch it."*

And one more.

> *Lucy pours Joyce a cup of coffee and then sits
> down at the kitchen table.*

"I'm running out of room around here. My food storage containers are spilling out of every cupboard," says Lucy, "and the ones I have in the fridge are taking up way too much room."

"You're in luck," says Joyce. "Suzie across the street is a RubberWare rep, and she's got some great products that take up almost no space. She's got RubberWare party coming up next week. We should go and pick up a few things."

"Sounds great," says Lucy. "You know, you almost sound like a commercial for Suzie!"

How do we find products and services? Sure, we have a bunch of search services literally at our fingertips. There's the Internet, and we still have the yellow pages, even if they are a shade of what they used to be. There are trade and service organizations that can help you select one of their members, and if you're looking for something in a strange city, your hotel might have a concierge.

> *Personal recommendations are the strongest means for delivering new business to a company.*

But many times, we simply take the word of someone else, friend or stranger. If they point us toward someone, we often follow their advice. Personal recommendations are the strongest means for delivering new business to a company. Overwhelmingly, we like to recommend the people who specialize in fixing the kinds of problems our friends are experiencing. If you want to add a deck to your house, we don't want to recommend someone who builds garages, we want to recommend someone who is an expert at building decks.

As a friend, we want to recommend experts to others. As a business person, we want to be the expert who gets recommended to others. We want to be that Recognized Expert.

A Recognized Expert is someone whom others believe to be the best in their industry or niche. They are known for their depth of knowledge on a particular subject. As the face of their business, they are known to provide superior products or services. They might have certifications and awards that provide proof of their expertise. Certainly they have people from their past successes that can testify to their prowess in their specialization.

A Recognized Expert can only be a person. You cannot create a fictional character for your business and "give" it RecEx Status. So developing RecEx Status is not for everyone. If you are timid, reclusive, and hate having your name in the media, you may not be the ideal RecEx for your business.

RecEx Status is very similar to other types of celebrity status, but instead of being known to the general public, a RecEx specializes in promoting their status within their industry or niche, and among their clients and potential clients. During a speech he was giving, I once heard a RecEx describe himself as "the most famous person people outside of this room have never heard of." That specialized celebrity is not cultivated just for the sake of free drinks or being asked for autographs. A RecEx uses her status to more easily reach their target market, and to earn greater profit from their work.

Many, many people have expertise in their field. Their knowledge may be unmatched by their competitors, the quality of their work unassailable. Many experts are not the head of the companies they work for, and they don't necessarily want to be the owner or CEO of a business. And that's just fine! At one time, I was a computer tech at a mid-sized environmental engineering firm. My "target market" was the 250 or so employees in the building where I worked. My focus was on convincing them that I was more knowledgeable about their computers and the

> *If you have expertise and no one knows it, are you really an expert?*

computer problems they experienced than my "competitor," the other computer tech with the company. I didn't care if anyone outside the company knew who I was.

The problem isn't necessarily "expertise," but in being

recognized for it by your competitors and your target market.
Very much like the tree falling in a forest, if you have expertise
and no one knows it, are you really an expert?

Benefits

The object of becoming recognized for your expertise is to
extend the reach and power of your existing marketing efforts.
The trappings of a properly implemented RecEx Status can help
tip a buying decision in your favor and reduce buyer remorse
after the transaction.

Unless you are the only person in your geographic region who
does your particular job, then you have competition. Imagine
what a potential consumer of your product or service goes
through to choose a supplier.

- Define exactly what they want

- Find a list of as many suppliers as possible

- Decide the differences between suppliers

- Attempt to discern the quality of the suppliers' products and
  services

- Ask for pricing and delivery

- Make a final decision on whom to go with

A properly crafted RecEx Status makes the job easier for the
prospective client. It can help them know right up front that
you're not the person for them. And that's actually a plus for
you, as your status helps potential customers self-qualify
themselves, and those that choose not to include you in their
decision process leave you more time to spend on true prospects.

The first problem prospects face is compiling a list of all
possible people who might be able to provide a solution to their
problem. Some businesses never get clients, because the
prospect pool never even finds out they exist. Not only do you
want to make it onto a prospect's radar, you want to be at the top
of the list. A RecEx can make it there.

Next, a prospect tries to figure out the major differences between possible suppliers. Whether they call it that or not, the prospect is trying to choose a *position* for each name on that list. Imagine a box, broken up into four quadrants. The vertical line in the center of the box is graduated from one extreme of a factor at the bottom, to the extreme opposite at the top. The horizontal axis is graduated from one extreme at the left to the opposite on the right. These factors are usually complimentary. The stereotypical positioning axes have "quality" as the vertical scale (low at the bottom to high at the top), and "price" as the horizontal axis (low at the left, high right). This is called a *position map*.

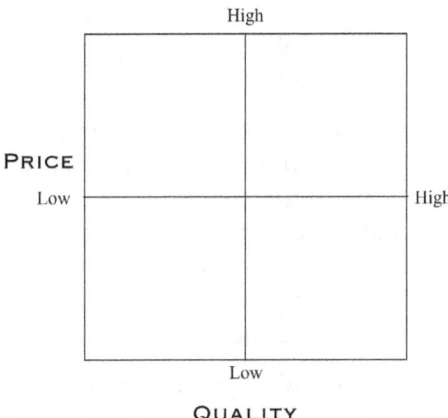

You want to use your Expert Proof Materials (EPM – more on those later), along with your other marketing tactics, to carve out a space on your prospect's position map where you have few or no direct competition. If you have no competition, and you're promoting the product or service the prospect is looking for, then you're probably going to get a call.

With competition, the prospect will have to consider other factors. Let's be blunt – all things being equal, they're probably going to flip a coin, or choose a popular name, or pick the closest company to solve their problem.

What you do not want is "all things being equal." You want to disrupt the playing field, put yourself on your own mountain towering over all your non-competitors. Ideally, you want to be introduced to the prospect by one of their friends as the best solution – the *only* solution – for their needs.

In the good old days of mass media, if it ever actually worked, the idea was that if a prospect saw a particular ad enough times, they would trot along dutifully and purchase whatever you were selling. The marketer was trying to compel members of the public to buy a particular whatsit.

> What you do not want is "all things being equal."

But the Holy Grail of marketing is the prospect's peer who, without being paid, recommends the marketer's product or service. When that happens, sales statistics go through the roof.

While your EPM and other marketing efforts will reaffirm your prospect's decision, it's being recommended as the expert that will make the sale. As a RecEx, you'll have dozens – perhaps hundreds or thousands – of unpaid salespeople running around and promoting you. Think of how much it costs to hire even one part-time sales person!

Once you've been recommended, you can present your EPM and other marketing materials. Unless the prospect is searching based solely on price (and no matter what you hear from other sales people and business owners, most aren't!), you have the opportunity to actually quote the prospect a higher price, and still make a sale.

Happy customers become happy non-paid salespeople, recommending you to others and thereby driving your sales numbers even higher. You have more people out and about selling for you, all the while earning higher profits.

And finally, with the combination of your EPM and your RecEx Status, you'll find yourself dealing with fewer sales prospects, people who need to be convinced to buy your product or service. You'll notice you're doing more "order taking" than "sales making" as your materials and RecEx Status do the selling for you.

With a carefully crafted and implemented RecEx Status, benefits include -

- Lower cost per sale
- Higher profits
- More sales coverage
- Pre-made sales

Doesn't this sound like something that's worth developing?

Expert Proof Materials

Originally the term masterpiece referred specifically to a piece of work by an apprentice or journeyman who wanted to become a master craftsman in the European guild system of the Middle Ages. That piece was often displayed in the guild house as evidence that the worker had sufficient skill and expertise to warrant being a master at his chosen craft.

Outside of the art world today, we don't often see people toiling over masterworks which will sit mutely, collecting dust. You need to produce something that -

- Demonstrates your deep knowledge and proficiency (aka expertise)
- Is something other experts are not doing
- Can be at least partially understood by prospects
- Is useful
- Can be replicated inexpensively or at no cost
- Can be easily distributed

Today, an EPM could be a print book or an ebook. It could be an educational class delivered on-line, or through a DVD or series of video clips on a web site. Digital is great, but if you can hand a prospect something that has physical dimensions and that takes up space on a book shelf or desk, something that they will actually look at, this is best.

One EPM is good, more than one is better. If you can produce materials for each level of prospect, that's the best yet.

Education

The surest way of moving a person from being a prospect to being a sale is to help them learn about their problem, and to educate them about your way of thinking. If you help them see the problem the way you do, and help them to understand why and how you implement your solutions, you stand a better chance of having them actually purchase from you.

At least one educational product is essential. Ideally this is a book or DVD, something a prospect can handle and hopefully read or watch. Backing up your main EPM, you should have other media. It might be a blog, or a series of articles you publish in magazines or newspapers. You should attempt to "touch" every medium available, including audio. There's a huge audience out there of people who listen to books and podcasts while traveling to and from work each day.

> You want to help align a potential customer's belief system with yours.

Whatever medium you use, the object of the piece should be to educate prospects about your industry or niche, and to bring them around to your way of thinking. You want to help align a potential customer's belief system with yours. You want your various EPM to examine your core subject from all angles.

Your educational materials should present several arguments for your point of view. You can make a drastic emotional statement ("The end of society is coming, and you need an underground shelter!" "You're ruining the value of your home with beat-up high end carpets."), but you can't leave it there. You should have a number of points to your argument, and explain each one in a way that either moves the reader, viewer or listener to your point of view, or reinforces their new understanding.

Don't be afraid to help the prospect accomplish something in your field by themselves. True, the overall object of producing educational EPM is to move the prospect to contact you and make a purchase. But some people will simply want to do things for themselves. If they succeed at a task by following directions you've set out in your EPM, they are more likely to promote you as the expert. Who could they have followed but the best in the field? They'll help find more prospects for your business.

Media

As I mentioned, there are a number of different media, all of which are now open to individuals because of advances in technology. It will take you very little effort to produce EPM in multiple formats. Here are just a few of the materials you can produce and distribute quickly and inexpensively.

- Print book
- Ebook
- DVD
- Web video
- Audio program
- Articles
- Blog

If you don't have the time to learn how to do something, there are any number of companies that will help you design a book, or record a podcast. You can even outsource 95% of everything, including – in some cases – the content of your EPM.

The Internet, with it's ability to replicate and deliver digital content, has revolutionized the production of media. Just a few years ago, if you had written a book there was the cost of paper, and the cost of having that paper printed, and then bound into volumes. Those books had to be stored somewhere, and then shipped to hundreds of book stores across the county. With an ebook, once the layout has been accomplished, there's no cost to replicate the book, or to send copies of a physical product to stores for eventual sales to individuals. Now, a person finds the book on Amazon, Barnes & Noble, or any one of a hundred other outlets. When they purchase a copy, they receive immediate access to a digital replica of the original. Even print books can now be economically reproduced one at a time, eliminating the cost of printing, storing and shipping hundreds or thousands of copies at once.

This is also the case with audio CDs and DVDs. There's still the cost of production, but duplication and distributing of the resulting media can again be accomplished via the Internet.

Periodicals – magazines and newspapers – are also being supplanted by web-based replica media. Many people now get their daily news throughout the day at outlets that combine previously exclusive "paper" or "TV" media into one outlet. Magazines are produced as digital products, in full color, with no duplication or distribution costs. And since these digital media no longer have to cater to a wide audience to support the costs of production and distribution, they can focus on narrower and narrower audiences, or niches.

As a result, it's easier to connect with a laser-targeted audience by seeking out and appearing in these niche media. Or even producing your own media, like emails or newsletters, that directly target the audience you're after. This allows you to get your EPM directly to the people you want to have experience it.

Public Relations

Once you've defined your target market, you'll use your marketing efforts to put yourself in front of them. Many people, however, don't fit into neat categories. They often don't do what others expect them to do, don't consume the same media others with the same interests do. You want to put yourself and your business in places where you'll be "tripped over" by people – places they don't expect to find you. This will help you find and connect with the market outliers.

The field of public relations now includes outlets like social media sites (Facebook, Twitter, etc,), blogs, as well as traditional and new news media. There are companies large and small that will help put you and your company in front of the public. I won't say you don't need one of these experts to help you. You may. Regardless, you need to understand a bit about the process.

> *You want to put yourself and your business in places where you'll be "tripped over" by people.*

There are many ways to get your message tripped over, many ways to get yourself found. The most basic is the media release. This is a news item sent out to targeted outlets. Many people will tell you that "news is not PR," and they're right. A news item details an important current happening. It doesn't cover persistent conditions of your business. It covers one current happening, sometimes topically and other times in depth, depending on the medium.

Very briefly, the best media releases you can put out don't promote you, but rather a client, vendor or member of the public, mentioning you and your product or service as a side note.

You can also write articles about your niche, and even opinion pieces that reach beyond your target market. You can participate in interviews that are recorded in text, audio, or on video and broadcast in various media. If you can, make sure that digital copies of these are archived on the Internet so that people doing searches can stumble across them.

You can make guest posts on other peoples' blogs, and contribute to discussions happening in various social media.

As with your other marketing efforts, the object of public relations is to promote you and your business in the best light. In this case you're moving beyond your industry and target market to place yourself in front of the general public. You want to earn recognition from the media and other institutions as an expert in your field. This will help you earn RecEx Status from others.

> Public
> relations is
> key to
> acquiring
> RecEx
>
> Status.

Public relations is key to acquiring RecEx Status. There's an entire section devoted to PR on our companion web site, ProfitAsAnExpert.com . I'll say it again: if you have expertise and no one knows it, are you really an expert?

All the effort you are putting in on PR is to bring you and your business to top-of-mind so that people will recognize you for your expertise, and recommend you to others.

RecEx Principles

These principles are the heart of becoming a Recognized Expert. Some of the major principles, Like the Epic Backstory, and some minor principles like Fans & Detractors, do not need to be developed first. But it's to your benefit to read and understand all the principles, and then apply them to yourself as you develop RecEx Status.

You may not use them all at first, but as you begin moving from working *in* your business to working *on* your business, perhaps by giving presentations or speaking in public before groups of prospects, you'll realize their worth.

Epic Backstory

Hero:
You must be the hero of your own story, taking responsibility for everything good and bad that happens to you. Outside forces may affect you, but final control rests with you.

Origin story:
You must have a repeatable story of your beginnings. It should be iconic – simple in words and imagery, easy to understand.

Heroic journey:
Your origin story must take you to higher highs and lower lows than an "ordinary" person. Listeners must be impressed and awed by both extremes.

Fatal flaw:

Superman was boring because he could not be beaten.
That's when the creators began using Kryptonite. Even
your fatal flaw must be bigger than life.

Restricted Access

Upstream communication barriers:

It must be difficult for your followers to talk to you, or to
see you in person. Downward communication – from you
to them – should be easy (for them) via books, videos,
courses & info from your inner circle.

Jargon:

A secret language, terms that "only the initiated can fully
understand" is essential. It makes your followers feel
included, and makes them feel like they're excluding
others. Some groups use long lists of specialized words
and acronyms, but just a few is good.

High costs:

Downward communication of basic information should be
easy and cheap (not free). Advanced information, training
courses, and face-to-face instruction should be increasingly
expensive in terms of cash and investment of time and
other resources. Value to an individual is proportionate to
what they have given up to get the information.

Hiding place:

You need a location where – and time when – you are
inaccessible even to your inner circle. Familiarity breeds
contempt. Inaccessibility breeds value. You should tell
your followers in general where your hiding place is *only* if

it inspires a desire to be in a similar place (private island, expensive hotel, etc.).

Exclusivity

Limited time:
Do not have an "open door policy" or "drop by any time" attitude. You can only be available to the masses during public appearances, which should be strictly limited in time and scope. Appear in cities they have to travel to, and only for X number of days or hours. Even your inner circle should have times when they cannot reach you.

Membership layers:
Base layer is farthest away (down) from personal contact. People who have read your books, seen your videos, taken your non-personal courses. They should aspire to the next layer, which is many-to-one face time (like personal instruction at a conference). Those people can aspire to closer association (few-to-one instruction). Each layer should have a higher and higher cost, which must consist of something other than – or at least in addition to – cash.

Purchase levels:
You should have multiple products or services with higher and higher costs. Mass products should be the least expensive, while the most expensive should be the most exclusive and the most difficult for an initiate to attain.

Differentiation:
"Our product/service/information is not like anything else out there. Our people (the initiates) are not like other

people. YOU are different, THIS is different, and here are
the differences. . ." (Flame broiled burgers VS square
patties VS not-a-burger sliced beef VS. . .). Helps develop
your position in the mind of prospects.

Do not sell:

Make info products (books, videos, online courses – Expert
Proof Materials) available to buy, but do NOT go selling
door-to-door (literally or metaphorically). Create "bait" for
potential initiates to consume and make them interested in
coming to you. Refusing to sell is both a way to
differentiate yourself from others and to set yourself above
them in the eyes of your prospects.

Repetition

People & place names:

Personal names make the story real. Failure to mention
names can make the listener feel subconsciously that you
are lying or omitting the truth. Specific numbers & dates
help.

High & low points:

Your heroic journey must be cathartic for your audience. It
must take them on a roller coaster ride. A large part of "the
experience of you" is entertainment.

Short:

Your heroic story must be easy for you and your listeners
to remember. It must be short and to the point, repeatable
by either of you in under one minute. However, you need a

medium-length and a longer version for more appropriate times.

Perseverance:

Your story (and most of your other marketing materials) will rapidly come to bore you, as they must not substantially change once you boil them down to the most effective version. You will become bored, but you must deliver the script each and every time as if you are excited to share it for the very first time. A prospect may have to hear your story a dozen times before it knocks down the wall of their resistance. Initiates will love repeating it for you to prospects and newer initiates. Your story is not for you, but for attracting prospects, and for reinforcing the correctness of an initiate's choice.

Trappings

Certification:

Being certified as genuine or important by an organization makes the information, product or service the initiate buys that much more valuable. Diplomas, awards, etc.

Fans & detractors:

You must have both fans and detractors, and acknowledge both. Detractors make your initiates feel more invested in having chosen you. Fans are your main marketing tool – they must talk about you, promote you, so that you can remain humble.

Uniforms & props:

Each membership layer should have its own uniform and/or accoutrements. Never be seen driving a cheap car if you're selling wealth. Never be seen in a suit if you're selling the simple life. From small to large, all trappings and clothes must match your message.

Definite opinions:

You must have definite opinions, and express them publicly. This is a way for your prospects to self-select – they either follow you or they don't. The ones that self-select for you are more likely to buy your higher-priced options. The ones who disagree with you may still talk about you, which is getting your message to an even wider audience.

Example

The Story of Dave

Dave Johnson ran a small rug cleaning business in Central City. He had a name for the business that told clients exactly what he did – *Dave's Superior Carpet Cleaning*. After doing some research on what other cleaners in the area charged, he determined that his rates were right in the middle – not too high, and not too low.

Dave had higher aspirations, though. He wanted to do better than just squeek by. He wanted to make enough money to support his family comfortably, but he also wanted to have the time to spend with them. Dave wanted to make more money than his competition, and work fewer hours. He saw some of the cleaning businesses in other cities with their large, flashy trucks and knew he could do just as well himself.

While Dave was looking for help, he came across ProfitAsAnExpert.com - Agile' Marketing's training system on increasing his wealth as a Recognized Expert. Dave looked it over and decided that the cost was worth it, and he'd give it a try.

EXCLUSIVITY

The first thing Dave did was to look at his target market. Originally, like his competitors, he saw everyone with a carpet as a potential client. But to work fewer hours and increase his income, he would have to focus on clients who could pay more, and who used a cleaning service on a frequent basis. As a result, he would have to narrow his marketing efforts. He would have to become more exclusive.

Dave looked into local carpet suppliers, and picked one that carried the highest-end carpet in the market. He went in and spoke with the owner, and told him honestly that he wanted an idea of where his high-end carpet was being installed. He offered to work with the dealer to offer a value-added service to his best clients. They worked out a deal where Dave would perform cleaning for the first year of the carpet's life, at no cost to the carpet owners. Dave had his first partner.

In return, Dave found out that in the past three years, one construction company had been installing the best carpet in the houses they built the Riverview development. This is where Dave decided to focus his efforts. He upgraded his work attire to a better uniform: crisply pressed chinos and a logoed dress shirt. He designed a new mailer that featured himself happily cleaning a high-end carpet.

CERTIFICATION

While he was getting other marketing aspects ready, Dave contacted the manufacturer of the highest-end carpet, Excelsior Carpets. They offered a program to certify anyone who took it to become an expert on their carpets. This certification also covered care and cleaning, so Dave invested some time and money in the course and within two weeks, he was a certified Excelsior Carpets expert. He incorporated this certification into his marketing efforts. He also went back to the original dealer and asked if he could quote the dealer as recommending him. The dealer agreed. Now Dave had two other experts who would certify that Dave was the person to go to for cleaning the highest-end carpets.

Dave took his newly-minted expertise to the local Home Builders Association. He offered to write articles on carpet cleaning for their monthly newsletter. In addition, he booked a booth at their annual Home Show in the spring. He was planning on using their attendance list to add to his marketing efforts, and to use his new expertise as a carpet cleaning columnist to add cachet to his marketing efforts.

REPETITION

Dave put together his new brochure. Instead of trying to target a nearly anonymous 50,000 people in and around Central City, he concentrated his first efforts on the trendy Riverview neighborhood. Dressing up in his best uniform, he visited the neighborhood and went door to door. Where people answered, he introduced himself and dropped off a packet that repeated his qualifications, as well his status as an expert on cleaning high-end carpets. He made a deal with one homeowner to clean their living room carpet for free in exchange for listing the owner as a satisfied client.

Dave also crafted a 12-week plan to hit and re-hit the area with mailings of his brochures. He knew that it took several exposures to an advertisement before it crossed into the conscious mind of the viewer. He would mail several invitations to the neighborhood, mentioning his web site and the number of his booking agent. His web site also repeated his bona fides as an expert on cleaning high-end carpeting.

RESTRICTED ACCESS

Dave had hired a phone service to act as his booking agent. Of course, he could concentrate on giving a client he was with his full attention. But the agent gave him another benefit. Potential clients would have to go though a chain of access (a short one, true) to get access to "Dave the expert." He realized that if anyone could get to him, at any time, he would no longer be literally in demand. He put together a list of the questions that were frequently asked of him, and wrote out standard answers. These FAQs he posted on his web site and added as a separate sheet in his printed marketing packet.

EXPERT PROOF MATERIALS

Dave compiled the articles he was writing for the Home Builders Association newsletter and, by adding a couple other short articles, he was able to put them together as a printed book. The articles, now chapters, outlined why keeping a high-end carpet clean was important, and why not just any cleaning process was best. Dave put a higher price on the cover of the book, made sure his picture and contact info was featured prominently on the back, then bought several dozen copies himself from the printer. He began to use these books as his business card, and to include them in the marketing package he gave to prospective clients.

He also arranged to be interviewed by local newspapers and trade association publications, and then copied those into his marketing kit. In addition, Dave did some video and audio interviews, and made them available on disk and on his web site. The book, the articles and the videos became his Expert Proof Materials, reinforcing with current and potential clients that he was, indeed, the go-to expert on cleaning high-end carpeting.

As a side effect of his expert status and limited availability, Dave was able to raise his prices to be some of the highest for any carpet cleaning service in Central City. This allowed him higher income from fewer hours of work each week. He was able to afford to upgrade his equipment more often, and to hire workers to do the actual cleaning while he spent time promoting the services his company offered.

Within just a couple of years, *Dave's Superior Carpet Cleaning* had gone from "also-ran" to becoming the one service that people wanted to hire to clean their carpets.

Action Items

1) What is your specialty? Something you do in your business better than anything else. Write it down.

2) Who is your ideal client or prospect? What do they do? Where do they live? What kinds of media do they view? Write down as detailed a description as possible. You are describing your target market.

3) What separates you from your competition? How are you different from others in your field? This is the position you want to occupy in your prospects' minds. Write it down, and then create a positioning map.

4) What can you teach your target market about your specialization? This might be a process, or information about a new product or service. Record this in some medium: text, audio, video, etc. This is your first educational EPM.

5) Do you have a diploma or certificate from an organization, stating that you meet a level of knowledge or experience? Can you get certified by an organization on your specialty? If so, work your certification into your marketing efforts.

6) How do the most successful people with your specialty dress while at work? What kinds of equipment do they have around them? Put together an appropriate uniform and accessories.

7) Solicit testimonials from satisfied clients. If you have to, write out what you want them to say and have them sign it. Get audio and/or video testimonials if possible.

Definitions

Brand: What each member of the public thinks about when they think of your company. Your brand exists only in the minds of as many people there are that think of you. Companies often try to influence their brands - what the public thinks of them.

EPM: Expert Proof Materials

Exponential: Not merely multiplied, but raised to a power. $3 \times 3 = 3 + 3 + 3 = 9$. $3^3 = 3 \times 3 \times 3 = 27$. Much stronger!

Marketing: The processes it takes to bring a favorable image of your business to the attention of your clients, your prospects, your industry, the media, and members of the general public. Can include media releases, advertising, presentations, publications, and much more.

Media Release: Information created by a business and presented to different media outlets. It contains news pertaining to the business and of possible interest to others. May be written, or in audio or video formats.

Positioning: How you and your business stand in the minds of your clients and prospects, in relation to your competitors. May be how they currently perceive you, or how you want to be seen.

Positioning Map: A visual representation of your current or intended position. Usually plotted on an X/Y axis, where the axes are different qualities being measured (ie - price and quality).

PR: Public Relations. In 2012, members of the Public
Relations Society of America established this definition:
"Public relations is a strategic communication process that
builds mutually beneficial relationships between
organizations and their publics."

RecEx: Recognized Expert. Someone seen by clients and
prospects as the go-to person in their industry or niche, and
recommended as such.

Target Market: The individuals who might most need or
want your product or service. These are the individuals
you try to engage with your marketing and public relations
efforts.

Top Of Mind: Coming first in customers' minds when
thinking of a particular industry or niche.

Word Of Mouth: Having clients or prospects mention
you, your business, your products or services favorably to
others. Ideally you want the "teller" to recommend a
purchase to the "listener."

Registering Your Book

I want to sincerely thank you for purchasing my book explaining *Recognized Expert Status*. If you found it useful, I'd ask that you do a couple things.

First, please register your copy at this address -

http://ProfitAsAnExpert.com/book-registration/

This will add you to a mailing list I keep **ONLY** for informing my readers about new books, or about major revisions to books I've published. You'll get a welcome email, and then emails only when I put out a new book.

Second, please take a moment and leave a review on-line. I hope if you found the book useful you'll leave a 4- or 5-star review.

Now, get to work on those action items and start building your RecEx Status today!